LET'S THINK ABOUT

the Power of Advertising

Elizabeth Raum

Heinemann
LIBRARY

Chicago, Illinois

Edited by John Paul Wilkins, Clare Lewis, and Kathryn Clay
Designed by Tim Bond and Peggie Carley
Picture research by Liz Alexander and Tracy Cummins
Production by Victoria Fitzgerald
Originated by Capstone Global Library Ltd

Library of Congress Cataloging-in-Publication Data
Cataloging-in-publication information is on file with the Library of Congress.
978-1-4846-0290-4 (hardcover)
978-1-4846-0295-9 (paperback)
978-1-4846-0305-5 (eBook PDF)

Photo Credits

Advertising Archives: 20, 22; Alamy: © ABN IMAGES, 8, © Asia Images Group Pte Ltd, 26, © BirchTree, 28, © Jeff Morgan_07, 25, © jeremy sutton-hibbert, 32, © Richard Wareham Fotografie, 19, © Todd Bannor, 33, © Wavebreak Media ltd, 27, © Zoonar GmbH, 13, © ZUMA Press, Inc., 34, 35; Corbis: © Bettmann, 14, © Swim Ink 2, LLC, 24; Dreamstime: © Americanspirit, 7; Getty images: Chris Ratcliffe/Bloomberg, 30, 31, kristian sekulic, 29, Mark Davis, 17, ranplett, 6, Robert D. Barnes, 41, Tetra Images, 38; Photo Researchers: 12; Shutterstock: Burlingham, 21 bottom, Gwoeii, 36, HomeStudio, 18, Monkey Business Images, 11, PKOM, 5, Sean Pavone, front cover, tehcheesiong, 21 top; Superstock: euroluftbild.de / F1 ONLINE, 43

Printed in the United States of America in North Mankato, Minnesota.
032017   010354RP

Contents

Some words are shown in bold, **like this**.
You can find out what they mean by looking in the glossary.

Advertising: What's the Issue?

We are surrounded by advertisements. Ads are plastered on buildings and buses. Ads appear in magazines and newspapers. Ads play on radio, TV, and at the theater. Huge billboards on the sides of roads advertise services and products to people passing by. Companies often print their names or **logos** on clothing and sports equipment. Sometimes T-shirts feature cartoon or film characters. That's a kind of advertising too. It draws attention to a particular TV show or film. Many websites carry advertisements. So do video games.

In this book, you'll explore the power of advertising. What is advertising? How does it work? Everyone seems to agree that we are surrounded by ads. Who creates them and how do they do it? Do ads change our behavior? If so, how?

Different views

Many people believe that advertising helps shoppers make good choices. Advertising creates jobs and helps businesses grow. Others claim that advertising causes more harm than good. It encourages people to buy more than they need. It adds to problems of waste and overspending. Some studies suggest that advertising is particularly harmful to children.

What do you think? Once you gather the facts, you'll be ready to form your own opinions and enter the debate.

DID YOU KNOW?

Design student Carolyn Davidson designed the now-famous Nike swoosh logo in 1971. She was paid $35 for her design.

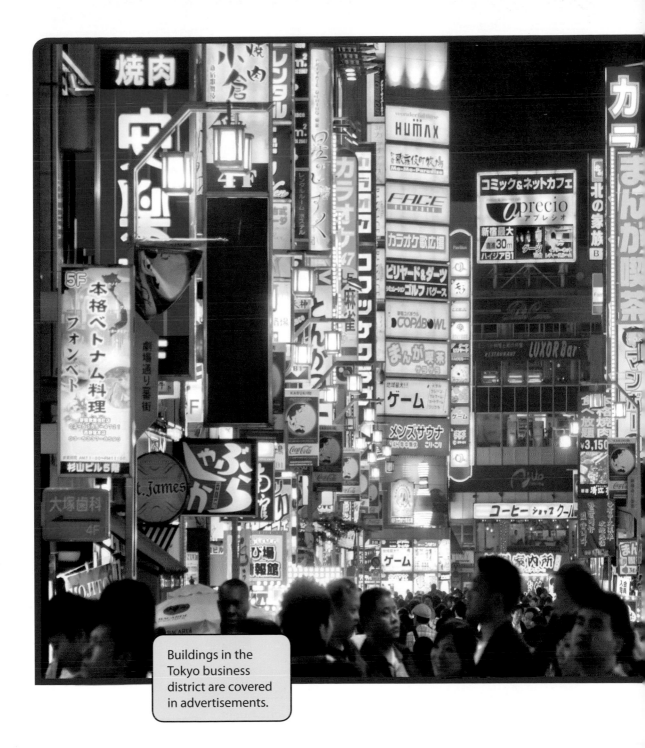

Buildings in the Tokyo business district are covered in advertisements.

What Is Advertising?

Have you ever made a poster to tell people about a special event? If so, you were advertising. Advertising is a kind of communication. Its purpose is to inform people about a particular event, idea, or product. Most advertising is designed to sell products and services. However, businesses are not the only ones who use advertisements.

Political ads

Politicians use advertisements to present their views and ideas. Political ads appear on TV, in newspapers and magazines, and online. At election time, political advertising increases. Politicians use buttons, banners, posters, and lawn signs to convince people to elect them to office. Politicians use advertising to reach voters in many different ways.

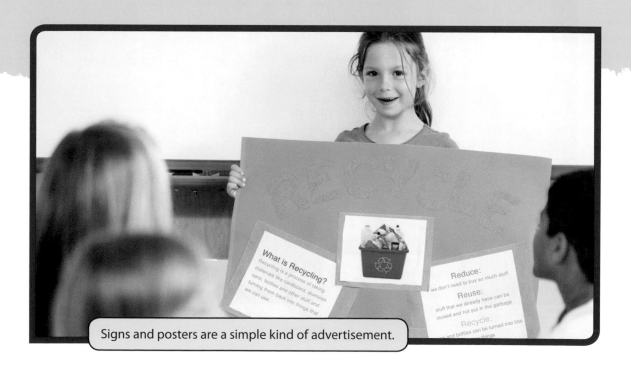

Signs and posters are a simple kind of advertisement.

Ads like this try to convince people to change their behavior.

Advertising for a cause

Many organizations and **charities** use public service ads. These ads tell people about certain causes, provide helpful information, or ask for donations. Ads like the one above try to convince people to change their behavior and stop smoking. Some public service ads encourage people to recycle, feed the hungry, and drive safely.

DID YOU KNOW?

In 1952 Dwight D. Eisenhower became the first U.S. presidential candidate to advertise on TV. His 30-second ads appeared during popular programs such as *I Love Lucy*. He spent $2 million on the ads. This equals about $18 million today. In 2012 President Barack Obama spent about $100 million on TV ads. Australia is considering banning political ads on TV because of the high costs. The United Kingdom, like many European countries, limits political advertising.

Selling a product

Most advertisements are designed to sell a product or service. Long ago people depended on friends or family members to tell them about new products. This kind of advertising—word-of-mouth or unpaid advertising—is powerful. We trust friends and family to give us good advice. If a friend tells you something is terrific, you are more likely to try it.

Companies want people to spread good news about their products. But they cannot depend on word of mouth, so they use many kinds of paid advertising. Newspaper and magazine ads are called print ads. At one time, print ads were the most common kind of advertising. Today companies spend more money on TV ads. They also advertise on the radio, in theaters, and online.

Ambient ads

Billboards, signs in stores or on streets, and ads on public buses are called **ambient ads**. Ambient ads, like the one below, are designed to catch your attention. They are often unexpected and get people talking about the ad and the product or service it offers. You'll find ambient ads in unusual places such as on clothing, receipts, sidewalks, or even at the bottoms of swimming pools.

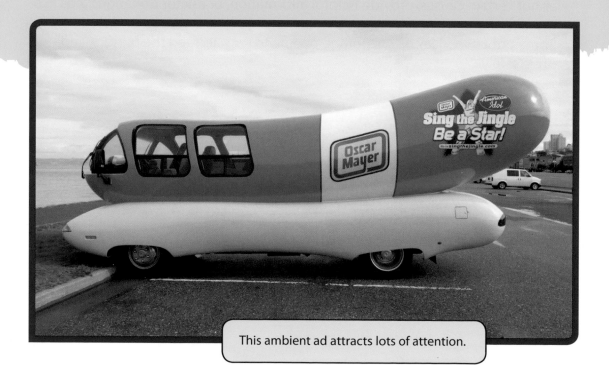

This ambient ad attracts lots of attention.

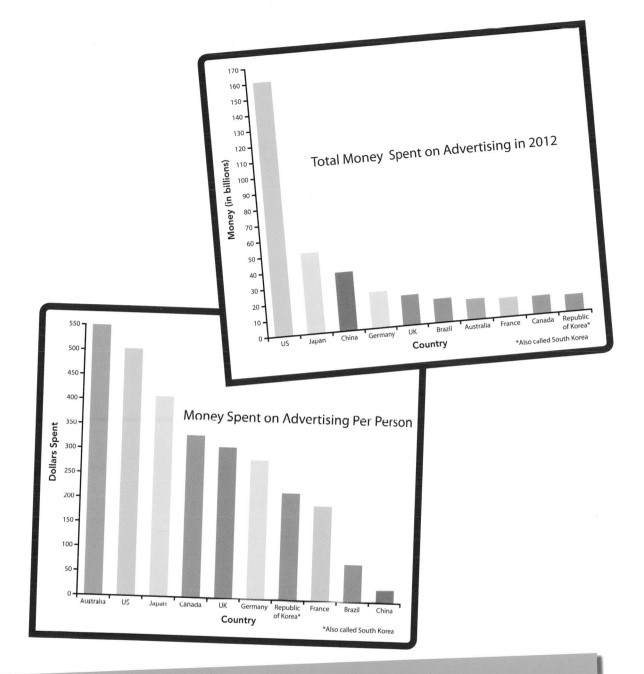

Total Money Spent on Advertising in 2012

Money (in billions) vs. Country: US, Japan, China, Germany, UK, Brazil, Australia, France, Canada, Republic of Korea*

*Also called South Korea

Money Spent on Advertising Per Person

Dollars Spent vs. Country: Australia, US, Japan, Canada, UK, Germany, Republic of Korea*, France, Brazil, China

*Also called South Korea

DID YOU KNOW?

In 2012 companies in the United States spent three times as much money on advertising as any other country. Australia spent the most on ads per person. China spent the least on ads per person. However, the amount of money Chinese companies spend on advertising is increasing more rapidly than any other country.

Online ads

More and more people depend on **digital devices**. So ads now appear on websites, cell phones, and video games. Many e-mail and social networking sites (such as Google, Yahoo, Facebook, and Twitter) keep track of the websites that people visit. This allows them to send **targeted ads** directly to users' accounts. For example, if you visit websites about bike racing, you might find ads for racing bikes when you log into your e-mail. If you search for information about new cars, new car ads may pop up when you go online.

Types of Advertising Today

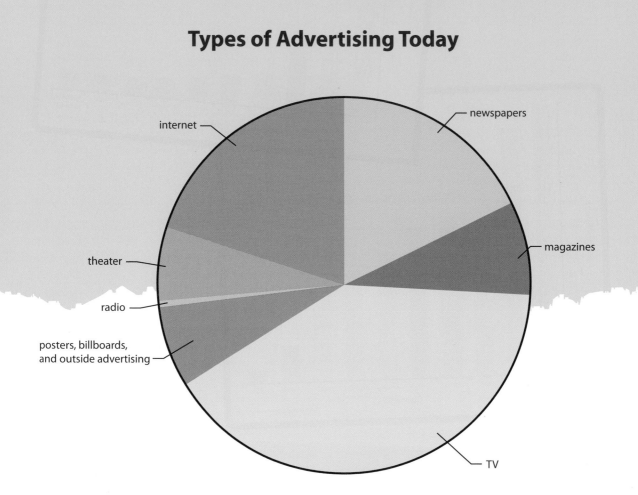

*Information is provided by the AA/WARC Expenditure Report, 2012

In-game advertising appears in the middle of some video games.

Product placement

Even video games have ads. Sometimes these ads are banners across the top or side of the screen. Other times the ads are hidden. Perhaps a character is drinking a certain **brand** of soda or eating at a fast food restaurant. This is called product placement. Product placements are also used in films and TV shows. When film or TV characters wear specific brands of clothes, use brand-name sporting equipment, or carry specific kinds of computers or cell phones, that is product placement. The advertisers make sure the brand names are easy to see.

WHAT DO YOU THINK?

Do you think that advertisers should be allowed to include their products in TV shows, movies, and video games? The next time you watch a TV show or movie, look for specific product placements. Keep track of how many you see.

The Importance of Advertising

In the past people grew their own food, built their own houses, and sewed their own clothes. They rarely traveled far from home. However, as the population grew and cities developed, people began depending on others for products and services.

Capitalism

In the United States, privately owned businesses provide goods and services. Businesses hire workers, purchase raw materials, and turn those materials into new products. Businesses pay their workers, and the workers can then use the money they earn to buy whatever they need or want. This system is called **capitalism**.

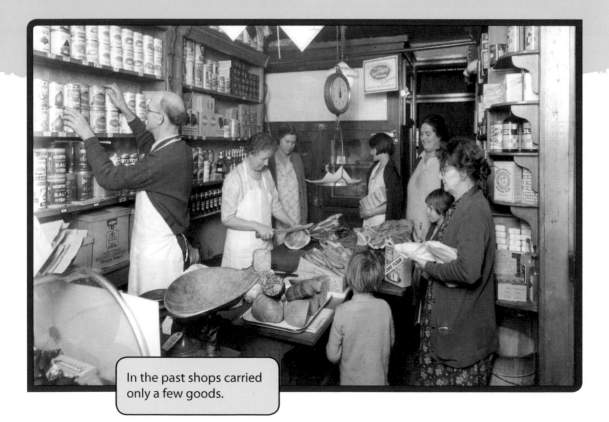

In the past shops carried only a few goods.

Under capitalism each person decides what to buy. People make decisions based on income, prices, and their likes and dislikes. This means that businesses must compete for customers. If businesses don't sell their products, they will fail. However, the more they sell, the bigger they will become. Advertising helps businesses make their products known and compete for customers.

WHAT DO YOU THINK?

A modern supermarket carries about 40,000 items. Even simple foods such as bread and milk come in different sizes and flavors. Some people think that life would be simpler with fewer choices. Others say that choices allow us to pick the products that are right for us. Think of a product, such as cereal, that offers many choices. What are the advantages of having choices? What are the disadvantages?

Today stores offer hundreds of choices.

Understanding needs versus wants

In a capitalist system each person makes decisions about what to buy. There are some things that everyone needs, such as nutritious food and warm clothing. There are other things we may want but can live without. These items are called wants or luxuries. Advertising appeals to both our need for basic items and our desire for luxuries.

DID YOU KNOW?

Advertising executive Gary Dahl made millions by convincing people to buy pet rocks. He began selling them in 1975. By the time the fad ended in 1976, Dahl had sold 1.5 million pet rocks for $4 each. Pet rocks are clearly a want.

	Examples of Needs	Examples of Wants
Drink	water	soda
Food	vegetables and fruits	cookies
Shelter	house or apartment	mansion or castle
Clothing	warm jacket	designer jeans
Activities	playing outside with friends; taking a walk	going snowboarding; going to the movies

The chart above gives clear choices. But sometimes our choices are more complicated. For example, is a bicycle a need or a want? A simple bike that you can ride to school may be a basic need for transport. An expensive racing bike may be something you want. It is important to know the difference. Understanding the difference between needs and wants helps us make good decisions about what we purchase.

WHAT DO YOU THINK?

Make a list of things you want. Put a check by those that are needs. Look at the ones that are wants. Why do you want them? Is your "want" reasonable? Why or why not?

Helping us decide what to buy

Companies hire advertising agencies to create ads and place them before the public. Marketing experts, artists, writers, photographers, and salespeople work in advertising. So do computer experts. An advertising agency usually develops an **advertising campaign** for a company. A campaign may include several different kinds of ads.

This simple model is one way advertisers decide what kinds of ads to create:

What?	Says what?	To whom?	In what media?	For what purpose?
What product or service does the company want to advertise?	What do they want to say about their product?	Whom are they trying to reach?	Will they use TV, print, online, or other media?	What is the hoped-for effect of the ad?
For example:				
ABC Ice Cream Bars	"Everybody loves ABC Ice Cream Bars."	children	TV	Children will want ABC Ice Cream Bars.

Advertising agencies must learn about the company and the company's potential clients. What message do they want to send? What is the best way to send that message? What is their purpose?

Got milk?

The "got milk?" ads were named one of the top 10 advertising campaigns of all time. They feature celebrities ranging from Superman to Taylor Swift. Each celebrity wears a milk moustache. The words "got milk?" appear below the picture. The ads were designed to convince people to choose milk over juice or soda. In a 2002 survey, 41 percent of Americans asked said they liked the ads "a lot," and 31 percent found them very effective. The result—people bought more milk.

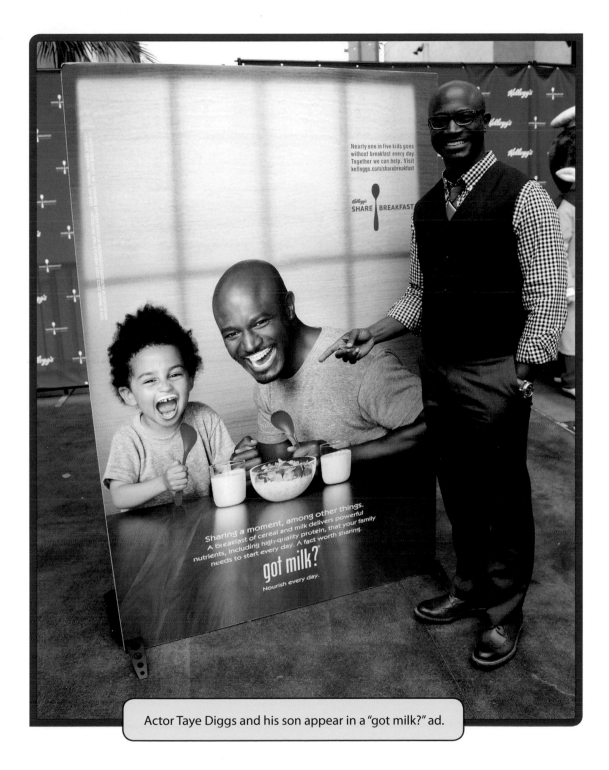

Actor Taye Diggs and his son appear in a "got milk?" ad.

How Advertising Works

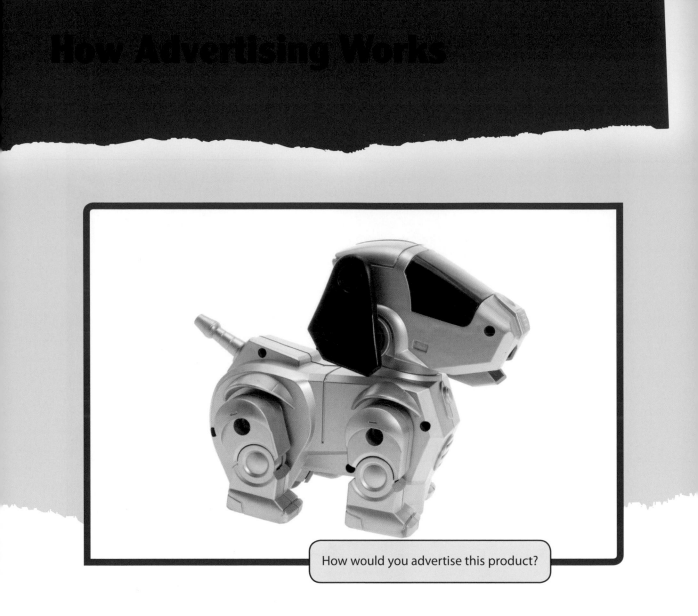

How would you advertise this product?

Imagine that you work for an advertising agency. You are asked to create an ad for the robot dog pictured above. You'll begin by considering the communication model. Will the advertisement work best if it is directed to children or to their parents? How will you reach the largest audience? Will a newspaper ad work better than a TV ad? Will you advertise online? These are the kinds of decisions that people in marketing make every day.

Creating a positive feeling

Advertisers don't expect us to rush out to buy their products the minute we see the ads. They know that advertising messages take time to sink in. Companies want to create positive feelings about their products so that we'll remember them in the future.

Even if we don't pay much attention to an ad, we may remember the **jingle** or music. An ad might make us laugh or smile. If we enjoy the ad, we may feel good about the product. That's the goal. The next time we go shopping and see hundreds of choices, we will probably choose a product we already feel good about.

DID YOU KNOW?

Most watches used in advertisements are set to 10:10. The hands often create a frame around the brand name and form a smiling face.

Advertising techniques

Advertisers use various methods or techniques to create positive feelings toward a product. Carefully planned photographs may make the product look tasty or fun. Advertisers may use facts and figures to prove that one product is better than another. For example, in a car advertisement they may include statistics about how much fuel the car uses per mile, or they may list all the safety features. Advertisers use humor to make us laugh and heart-warming stories to make us feel good about a product.

After the show, we always show up at McDonald's

Summer appetites really get big after the sun goes down. And when your stomach starts talking, McDonald's has the answer. Big Mac' or Filet-O-Fish' Sandwiches. Shakes. Sundaes and McDonald's world famous fries are some of the delicious menu choices McDonald's offers you. With fast, friendly service and prices that fit any family budget, McDonald's "sure is good to have around."

McDonald's

You deserve a break today

This advertising campaign for McDonalds was voted "jingle of the century" in 1999. The ad helped McDonald's increase global sales by millions of dollars.

The truth effect

Have you noticed how the same products are advertised over and over? You begin to learn the jingles. You may even memorize the words of the ad. Advertisers know that when ads are repeated, they begin to seem true. This is called the "truth effect." Effective jingles, such as the McDonald's jingle, ring true. Who would say that they don't deserve a break? Ads can draw us to a product through repetition and the appearance of truth.

Seeing is believing

The burger on the top appears in advertisements. It was specially made to look good in photographs. In truth, it probably wouldn't fit into its box. The one on the right looks more like what you'd get at a fast food restaurant. Why is there a difference between the advertised burger and the real burger? Can you trust the things you see in advertisements? How do you know which ads to believe?

Appeals that work

In addition to creating positive ads and repeating them, advertisers appeal to people's basic desires and emotions. For example, most people want to be healthy, have fun, and avoid embarrassment. The chart below shows some of the most common appeals used in advertisements. Different products require different appeals. Advertisers choose the appeals carefully depending on the product and the audience.

profit	Can the product save you money?
health	Will it make you healthier?
love or romance	Will it increase your chances of finding a boyfriend or girlfriend?
fear	Can this product save you from embarrassment, illness, growing old, or looking bad?
admiration	Does someone you admire use this product?
convenience	Will this product or service make your life easier?
fun and pleasure	Is it fun?
vanity	Will it make others admire you?
environmental concern	Does it help the environment?

A closer look

Imagine that an advertising agency is preparing an ad for a new kind of soap. Advertisers might use the **profit** appeal to convince adults that this brand will save them money or the health appeal to report that this soap will kill germs. The advertiser may emphasize that using this soap is fun when advertising on children's TV. The advertiser may use a popular singer (**admiration**) to appeal to teenagers. Advertisers may use more than one appeal in a single ad.

WHAT DO YOU THINK?

Can any product really solve all your problems or fulfill all your desires? Do you think that using a particular product will make you more popular? Why or why not?

TODAY
Thinking green

TOMORROW
Planning for blue

TOYOTA
toyota.com/future

Can today's environmental thinking inspire tomorrow's technology? Toyota believes so. Since its launch, the Prius has earned the love of millions of forward-thinking drivers. We estimate our hybrid technology has saved a billion gallons of gas and lowered CO_2 emissions by billions of pounds.* It's also paving the way for the next generation of environmental vehicles. Like cars charged at home. Or cars that will run solely on electricity, or consume hydrogen and emit only water. Because when it comes to thinking green, the sky's the limit.

*Estimated savings compares each U.S. hybrid vehicle's EPA combined mpg rating with its segment average based on latest EPA Trends Report (driven 15,000 miles annually). Actual mileage will vary. ©2009

This advertisement appeals to drivers who care about the environment.

How Advertising Helps Us

Advertising is an important part of the **economy**. Thousands of people are employed in the advertising industry. Many experts believe that advertising helps individuals, the country, and the world.

Advertising creates jobs

Advertising helps companies increase sales and leads to higher profits. Higher profits help companies grow. Growing companies buy raw materials, build new factories, and purchase other services. They also hire more workers who then have more money to spend. The economy becomes stronger when people have good jobs.

In the past vehicle advertisements used different appeals. What appeal is being used in this ad?

Helping the world economy

Many companies now sell products all over the world. One example is Procter & Gamble (P&G). P&G makes 300 different brands and sells products to almost 5 billion customers in 180 countries. Many of the world's most powerful brands, such as Apple, Microsoft, and Coca-Cola, hire workers all over the world. The workers earn money that they spend in their own countries, which helps those economies grow stronger.

Encouraging new product development

Advertising encourages companies to develop new and better products. Companies count on advertisements to draw attention to their new inventions or improvements in older products. Some products fail, of course. But others last forever.

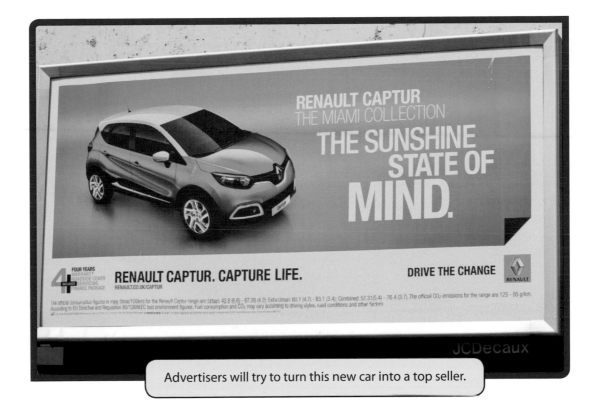

Advertisers will try to turn this new car into a top seller.

Growing business

According to a study in the United Kingdom, money spent on advertising helps the economy. This does not mean that every ad increases a company's sales. Some ads work; others do not. Instead, the study shows that advertising has a positive effect on business.

Presenting choices

Advertising doesn't just introduce new products. It also presents a full range of choices. Ads may offer additional information about a product. How does it work? What does it cost? What special features does it include? This information helps people make better choices. Advertising encourages people to compare products by considering size, style, price, options, and quality.

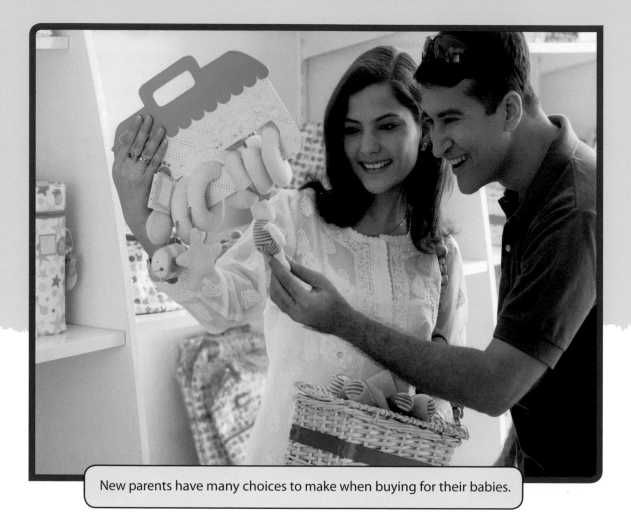

New parents have many choices to make when buying for their babies.

Making shopping convenient

Today many people are buying products and services online. By looking at company websites and online shops, they can find what they need without leaving home. Experts expect online shopping to increase dramatically in the coming years.

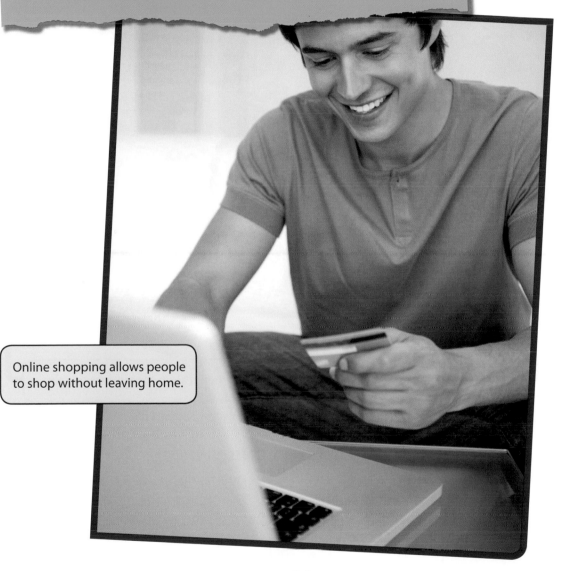

Online shopping allows people to shop without leaving home.

Providing new business opportunities

Online advertising makes it possible for individuals to market their own products. The website Esty provides a place for people to market handmade items. People who make toys, jewelry, clothing, food items, and much more can now sell their products online. This is easier and cheaper than opening an ordinary shop.

Advertising lowers prices

In order to sell more, companies may lower prices or offer sales. A well-known study showed that advertising reduces prices even without special sales. That's because the more items a company sells, the less it costs to make each one. This is called **economy of scale**. Companies pass the savings on to customers.

Advertisements alert **consumers** to sales.

Advertisements support important causes

Sometimes businesses include charities in their advertising. In 2012 Marks & Spencer designed a marketing campaign called "shwopping." Their ads urge shoppers to leave an older item when they buy something new. Marks & Spencer's provides "shwop drops" in its stores. The store sends the older items to Oxfam, an agency that helps the poor. The items are then given to people in need. These advertising campaigns increase sales and help others. However, some people believe it is better to give money or goods directly to charities. Many charities and other organizations create their own public service ads to reach the public. Stores or companies may make it easy to give to charity, but their real goal is to increase their own sales.

Bigger and better?

You can test the idea of economy of scale at the supermarket. Compare the cost of a giant box of cereal to the cost of the smallest box of the same cereal. Which one costs less per serving? Test other products. Does buying more reduce the price per serving? Remember that bigger is not always better—especially if the item might go bad before it is used.

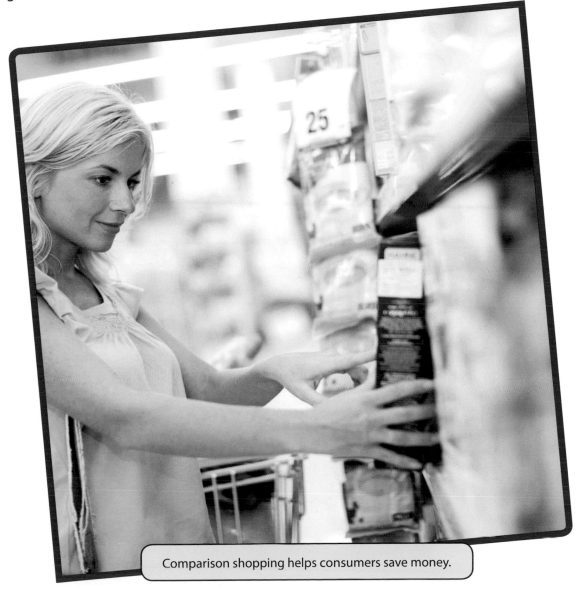

Comparison shopping helps consumers save money.

Advertising supports entertainment

TV networks charge large fees to advertisers. These fees are used to support programming and other TV costs. In 2011 the average price of a 30-second ad on TV was $108,956. Sporting events, such as the 2012 Olympics, depend on the money from TV advertising. Major TV network NBC sold more than $1 billion worth of ads to broadcast during the Olympics. The money is divided between the TV network and the Olympic committee.

Newspapers and magazines also depend on advertising money. Without advertising, the newspapers would have to double their prices. Today many newspapers and magazines publish articles online. The ads appear online as well.

Companies pay a lot of money to show their ads during popular sporting events.

Advertising supports websites

Many websites use ads to help pay the costs of running the site. Companies pay a fee to the website owner each time someone clicks on their ad. Sometimes the website owner is an organization, school, or individual. Not everyone is pleased about all the ads on websites. But the ads can be an important source of money for some organizations.

How Advertising Causes Harm

Some people believe that advertisements are harmful. They point to advertisements that deceive us. Some advertisements are misleading. Common ways advertisers mislead consumers include:

• weasel words that suggest a positive meaning without really making any guarantee that can be measured. Phrases such as "people say," "most people agree," and "studies show" are weasel words.

• the bandwagon technique, which is the suggestion that everyone else is using the product so you should too. Celebrity ads may also use this technique. Just because a celebrity is using the product does not mean you should.

• glittering generalities that use appealing words and images to sell the product. For example, the product will "change your life" or turn you into a "cool kid." Again, this cannot be proved.

Making false claims or lying in ads is illegal. Companies cannot say that a medicine cures an illness unless there is scientific proof that it does so. However, misleading advertisements are not illegal. It is up to consumers to read or watch ads closely and make their own judgements.

Advertisers use celebrities to promote products.

Be ad aware

A candy store at the local shopping center posts a big sign in the window that says "World's Best Chocolates." Are they really the best in the world? There is no way to prove or disprove the claim. This kind of advertising is called puffery. It is not against the law. The shop is stating an opinion, not trying to deceive customers.

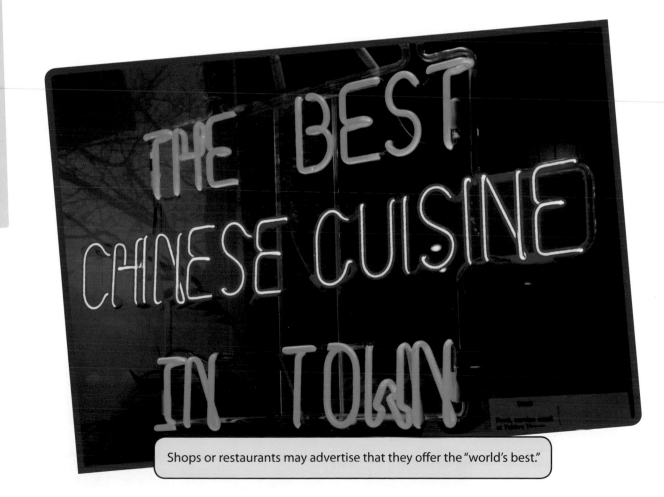

Shops or restaurants may advertise that they offer the "world's best."

Advertising causes us to want more

Advertising creates a demand for more and better things. "New and improved" are words often used in ads. This leads us to think that what we now have is not good enough. Advertising may convince people that the things they want are actually things that they need. For some people, shopping becomes a habit that has little to do with their basic needs. Advertisements convince them to buy more. Studies show that unhappy adults believe that owning more things will make them happier. They buy things but still feel unhappy. So they buy even more. It can become a never-ending cycle.

Advertising may lead us to buy things we don't need and can't afford.

Advertising leads to overspending

Advertising may lead some people to overspend. Items on sale seem too good to miss. Some shoppers get so excited that they buy more than they can afford and more than they need. Some sales advertise "buy two get one free." It may be a good deal. But if you only need one, why buy two? Consumers should think carefully before they buy.

Many people today use credit cards. This habit makes it easy to overspend. The result is that millions of people are in debt. They owe more money than they have. Advertising, especially by credit card companies, makes it easy to spend money. Unfortunately, it's not easy to get out of debt.

WHAT DO YOU THINK?

Children's writer Maurice Sendak once said, "There must be more to life than having everything!" What things are more important than material goods?

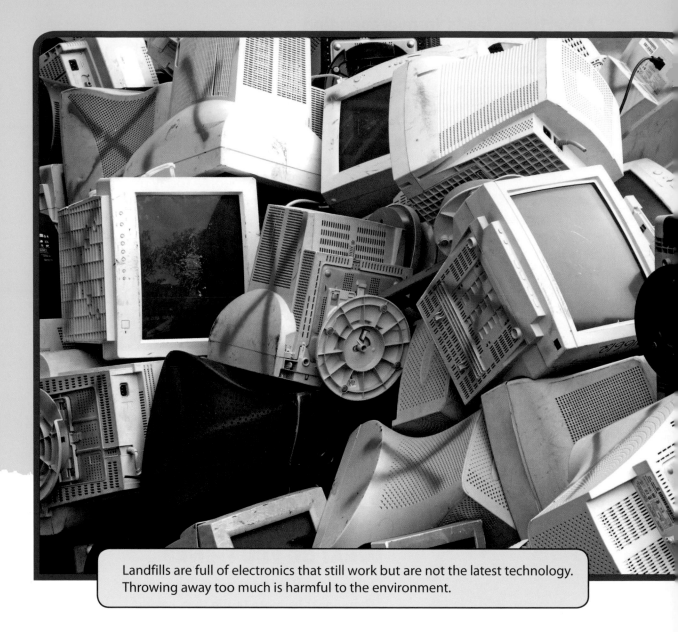

Landfills are full of electronics that still work but are not the latest technology. Throwing away too much is harmful to the environment.

Advertising leads to waste

If advertising leads to overspending, then it also leads to waste. We've become a throwaway society. We replace old but still usable objects with brand new ones. We toss the old ones away. This practice is not just wasteful. It's also dangerous. Plastics, electronic equipment, and other waste products release dangerous chemicals that may cause illnesses. Advertising may be partly to blame for the piles of trash in the world's landfills.

Ads are annoying

Many people think ads are annoying. In a recent survey, 91 percent of Americans reported being annoyed by ads. As many as 43 percent said they would ignore any company that sends them two or more online ads or **spam** e-mails. Even so, the ads may influence what they buy. Of course, people can turn off the TV or stop buying newspapers and magazines. But some ads are unavoidable. Ambient ads surround us. Online ads appear with every click of the mouse.

How Consumers Feel About Advertising

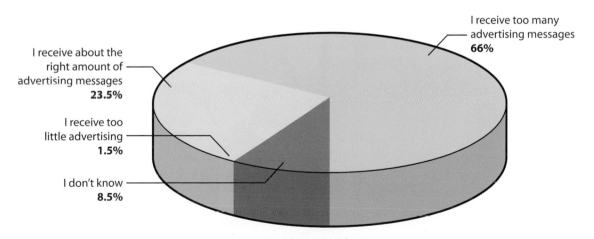

I receive too many advertising messages
66%

I receive about the right amount of advertising messages
23.5%

I receive too little advertising
1.5%

I don't know
8.5%

A 2012 survey asked people in the United Kingdom and the United States how they felt about the amount of advertising they received via e-mail, text messages, websites, and other digital sources.

Advertising to Children

Many advertisers target children. They not only sell items that appeal to children, but they know that children influence what their parents buy. Children up to age 11 spend more than $31 billion of their own money each year. Teenagers (ages 12 to 19) spend more than $872 billion. Some reports suggest that children and teenagers have a big influence on their parents' spending each year. Considering this huge amount of money, it is not surprising that advertising to children is increasing. Today advertisers spend more than $17 billion per year advertising to children and teens.

Many ads aimed at children suggest that certain products will turn them into cool, popular kids.

Surrounded by ads

Children and young people have greater access to TV and computers today than in the past. In the United Kingdom about 70 percent of children ages 8 to 18 have a TV in their bedrooms. This means that they are watching TV without their parents' supervision. Children are online, playing video games, and using cell phones. Some advertisers even buy space at schools, putting ads on gym floors, in buses, or in hallways.

WHAT DO YOU THINK?

Advertisers studied nagging and discovered that children ages 12 to 17 usually ask parents for a product about nine times before the parents give in. Many ads directed at children and teenagers encourage them to nag their parents to buy particular products. Do you think decisions based on nagging are good decisions? Why or why not? If not, who is to blame—parents for giving in, children for nagging, or advertisers for encouraging nagging?

Program or ad?

Studies show that children under age 8 cannot tell the difference between an advertisement and a TV program. They are not able to make good judgements. Older children know the difference between nutritious food and junk food, but younger children do not. If an ad claims that sugary cereals are healthy, young children believe it, especially if a favorite character says it is true.

Party, game, or ad?

Advertisers know the power of word-of-mouth advertising, so they sometimes use children to advertise products to other children. This is called peer-to-peer marketing. For example, a company may sponsor a children's party. The host child invites friends to come and try a new product such as nail polish or sports equipment. It may feel like an ordinary party, but it is really advertising.

Events and contests may be hidden advertisements too. A store may hold a special event with games and activities to encourage children to buy a certain brand of sports equipment. Restaurants may give out vouchers as prizes for school contests. This kind of hidden advertising occurs online too. Companies sponsor activities, games, and contests that include ads and use product placement.

WHAT DO YOU THINK?

Sweden and Norway forbid advertising aimed at children younger than the age of 12. Denmark and Belgium limit advertising to children. Do you agree with them? Should the government ban advertising to children?

Some people believe that advertising should not be allowed on children's TV programs.

The Future of Advertising

Advertising keeps changing to reflect how people shop and communicate. Online advertising is increasing rapidly. Advertisers will find ways to make ads more fun and less annoying. For example, future online and cell phone ads may flash across screens and disappear.

Viral advertising

Advertisers will increase peer-to-peer marketing. Viral ads are a form of peer-to-peer marketing. Companies create funny videos and use celebrities to sell their products. These short video ads may spread like a virus when people forward them to friends. When that happens, they are called viral videos. Recently Samsung Corporation hired Jay-Z and Usher to make short video ads. The videos reached millions of viewers because people sent them to friends.

How Much Countries Spend on Online Advertising
(in billions)

Country	2011	2012	2013 (est.)	2014 (est.)
United States	32.0	39.5	46.5	52.8
Japan	7.21	8.10	9.58	10.17
United Kingdom	7.13	7.91	8.70	9.70
Germany	5.16	6.59	7.42	8.62
China	4.57	6.21	7.63	9.46
France	2.88	3.20	3.50	3.95
Canada	2.16	2.54	2.86	3.23
Italy	1.52	1.78	2.01	2.27
Spain	1.20	1.41	1.48	1.67

Targeted ads

Shops target individual consumers by providing them with loyalty cards to use when paying for their goods. These cards track what shoppers buy. Shoppers may get vouchers or e-mail ads for these products. This kind of targeted advertising is sure to increase, especially online.

Reaching new populations

Online advertising, cell phone apps, and product placement is not limited by geography. Advertisers will reach out to new consumers around the world. Advertisers are particularly targeting Chinese consumers. China has a huge population and a growing economy. Some ads, like the one below, are not even limited to people on Earth!

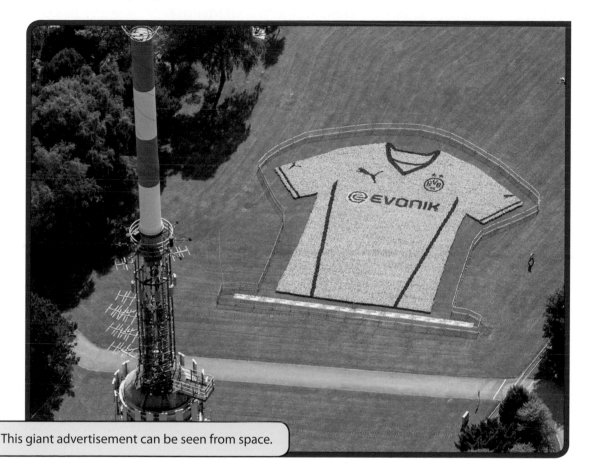

This giant advertisement can be seen from space.

WHAT DO YOU THINK?

Do you think it is appropriate for companies to track the websites you visit? Why or why not?

Debate It!

Are you ready to debate some of these issues with your friends?
If so, these five tips may help.

1. Be prepared. Do some research before you begin. Make a list of points you plan to debate. Then think of arguments on the other side. That way you'll be prepared when your friend mentions them.

2. State your opinions clearly. It's useful to provide examples and statistics.

3. Listen carefully. After all, you cannot respond effectively unless you understand exactly what your friend is saying. You can ask your friend to repeat the comment or provide further information.

4. Keep your cool. In a good debate there is no clear winner or loser. You will win some points and lose others. You may even find that some of your friend's comments make sense. That's not bad. It shows that you are keeping an open mind.

5. Have fun! Debate is a great way to explore the issues.

Glossary

admiration act of liking and respecting something or someone

advertising campaign series of advertising messages that share a single idea or theme

ambient ad ad placed in an unsual place or on an unusual item

brand name that identifies a product

capitalism economic and political system in which private owners control a country's trade and industry

charity organization that provides help or raises money for those in need

consumer person who buys things

digital device electronic device, such as a cell phone

economy wealth or resources of a country or region

economy of scale savings in the cost of producing goods due to an increase in the number of items produced

jingle short verse or song with catchy repetition

logo symbol that represents a company or brand that is designed to be easily recognizable

profit financial gain

spam electronic junk mail

targeted ad ad aimed at a specific audience

Find Out More

Books

Burstein, John. *Big Fat Lies: Advertising Tricks*. Slim Goodbody's Lighten Up!
New York: Crabtree Pub., 2008.

Connolly, Sean. *Advertisements*. Getting the Message. Mankato, Minn.:
Smart Apple Media, 2010.

Green, Jen. *Advertising*. Ethical Debates. New York: Rosen Central, 2012.

Hensley, Laura. *Advertising Attack*. Mastering Media. Chicago: Raintree, 2011.

Wittekind, Erika. *The Big Push: How Popular Culture Is Always Selling*. Exploring
Media Literacy. North Mankato, Minn.: Compass Point Books, 2012.

Websites

"Don't Buy It: Get Media Smart"
pbskids.org/dontbuyit
This Public Broadcasting Service (PBS) website teaches young people
how to be savvy consumers.

"Duke University Libraries: Ad* Access"
library.duke.edu/digitalcollections/adaccess/
Check out this Duke University website to see a wide range of
advertisements from 1911 to 1955.

"You Are Here"
www.consumer.ftc.gov/sites/default/files/games/off-site/youarehere/index.html
This website shows how young consumers are affected by advertising.

Further research

- Keep a log of advertising for one 24-hour period. Write down how many ads you see, where you see them, and what appeals they use to get your attention. Share this with your family and friends.

- Develop an advertising campaign for a cause in which you believe. Choose a target audience, the type of media you will use, and the appeals that will work best to promote your cause.

- Research one product. How much money does the company spend on advertising each year? Where do they advertise? What kinds of appeals do they use? Do you think the ads are effective? Why or why not?

Index